How to
REACH YOUR
FULL POTENTIAL
for GOD

STUDY GUIDE

Charles F. Stanley

THOMAS NELSON
Since 1798

NASHVILLE DALLAS MEXICO CITY RIO DE JANEIRO

Published in Nashville, Tennessee, by Thomas Nelson, Inc. Thomas Nelson is a registered trademark of Thomas Nelson, Inc.

Library of Congress Cataloging-in-Publication Data Available

ISBN 978-1-4002-0272-0

Printed in the United States of America.

09 10 11 12 13 RRD 5 4 3 2 1

TABLE OF CONTENTS

INTRODUCTION

Are you excited about your life and who God created you to become? Are you eager to take up the path He has set out for you? Perhaps you are. But it's possible you've chosen this study because you need assurance that there is more to life. Maybe you are going through a difficult season with no apparent end to your trials. Or maybe you lack purpose, direction, and hope for the future. Whatever the reason, one thing is certain: you have not found this workbook by coincidence. God has brought you to this point for a reason. He wants you to experience the awesome fullness of a life centered in His love, in line with His will, and dependent upon His provision. But this cannot happen apart from an intimate relationship with Him.

God will reveal Himself and His plans to you as you follow Him through life's many challenges—not only in major decisions, but in many other ways. Walking closely with the Lord is fundamental to discovering and fulfilling His calling on your life. By learning to submit to His will, your relationship with Him will grow deeper and more satisfying as time passes. Remember, God knows His children better than they know themselves, and you are no exception. He alone is capable of bringing out the best in you.

It all starts with receiving Jesus Christ as Lord and Savior. You cannot know God intimately without first accepting the One who reconciles you to the Father. As Romans 5:10 tells us, "While we were enemies we were reconciled to God through the death of His Son, much more, having been reconciled, we shall be saved by His life." Through Jesus' death on the cross, and the power of His resurrection, we are restored to a right relationship with the Father. He is our king, savior, healer, and the means by which we enter the kingdom of God.

Romans 10:9 makes a promise. It says, "If you confess with your mouth Jesus as Lord, and believe in your heart that God raised Him from the dead, you will be saved." Your creator loves you unconditionally and desires for you to experience the profound depth of His care. Why wait? Tell God, in your own words, that you are willing to trust Him for salvation and live according to His principles, or use the following prayer:

Lord Jesus Christ, have mercy on me. Please forgive my sins and save me from spending eternity apart from Your life-giving love. By faith, I accept the work You accomplished on the cross as a worthy sacrifice for my transgressions. Thank You for providing a way to know You intimately and grow in relationship with my heavenly Father. I gratefully receive Your gift of eternal, abundant life with open arms. Thank You for hearing my prayer and for loving me unconditionally. I ask now for the strength, wisdom, and determination to walk in the center of Your will from this day forward and to become all You created me to be, for Your glory. Amen.

Congratulations! By praying this prayer you have received Christ as your Savior, and your life will never be the same. I would love to know about your new relationship with the Lord. Please contact In Touch's Customer Care Center at (800) 789–1473 so that we can rejoice with you. We'll also send our *New Believer's Kit* to you as a free gift.

DO YOU WANT GOD'S BEST?

Read Chapter 1 of *How to Reach Your Full Potential for God*

Scripture Passage: Joshua 1:1–9

THINK ABOUT TODAY

The dictionary defines *potential* as a "latent excellence or ability that may or may not be developed." According to that definition, where do you fit in? Have you identified and nurtured your abilities or left them undiscovered and dormant? Perhaps you struggle to believe there is any potential within you at all.

1. Take a few moments and, in twenty-five words or less (and without taking more than five minutes), describe what you believe is your God-given potential.

_____

_____

2. In your opinion, what are three things required of someone who wants to reach his or her full potential?

   1. _____
   2. _____
   3. _____

3. Consider your reasons for participating in this study and respond to the following questions:

   • What do you want to discover about God?

   _____

   _____

   • What do you want to learn about yourself?

   _____

   _____

   • How will you put into action your newly acquired knowledge?

   _____

   _____

THINK ABOUT GOD

"The truth is, many people are not pursuing their potential. They are not factoring God into their decision-making or into their goal setting. They cannot clearly and succinctly say what they believe to be God's foremost purpose and plan for their lives. They will stare at you blankly if you ask, "What do you believe to be God's will for you?" (p. 5).

1. While in the decision-making process, when do you typically consider asking God for help?

   __ long before it's time to make the decision

   __ in the midst of making the decision

   __ after the fact, if things didn't go as planned

   __ never

2. Take some time to read and react to the four main truths mentioned in this chapter. As you reread them, consider how true they are based on your lifestyle. It's one thing to agree that something is true, but it is another to put that truth into action.

a. God has a plan and purpose for your life.

Do you believe this is a true statement?

   __ yes

   __ no

Explain your response.

_____

_____

_____

Mark the line below to indicate the degree to which you are actively and consistently engaged in living out God's purpose for your life.

Not at all ⟵————————————————⟶ All the time

What prevents you from pursuing God's will?

___ I don't know what it is.

___ I'm afraid to follow through.

___ My life is too comfortable right now.

___ My relationship with God isn't strong enough.

___ Other: _____

b. God has already endowed you with the gifts and talents you need to complete the work that He has assigned, prepared, and provided for you to do.

Do you believe this is a true statement?

___ yes

___ no

Explain your response.

_____

_____

_____

_____

How do you know what your gifts and talents are?

_____

_____

_____

When you put your abilities to work, are they for your benefit or for the Lord's? Explain your response.

_____

_____

_____

How does your relationship with God affect the way you employ the gifts and talents He gave you?

_____

_____

_____

c. *Nobody on earth can be who you are, replace you, or fulfill God's plan for your life.*

Do you believe this is a true statement?

___ yes

___ no

Explain your response.

_____

_____

_____

If the Lord has a plan for your life, then you are instrumental to His purposes. What happens when you fail to accomplish God's will?

_____

_____

_____

Are you presently fulfilling your divine purpose, or is someone else covering your role? Explain your response.

_____

_____

_____

d. *You must establish firm commitments in various areas of your life in order to pursue and begin to reach your God-given potential.*

Identify your most significant obligations. Do any of these receive more time than your relationship with the Lord?

_____

_____

_____

What commitments does God want you to give up, if any?

_____

_____

_____

Which need more attention?

_____

_____

_____

How do your commitments affect pursuing God's plan and purpose for your life?

___ Not at all; I'm focused on God's plan.

___ I go back and forth between my plan and God's plan.

___ I am totally committed to my plans and fit God into my schedule when possible.

Does your life's present direction lead you toward or away from accomplishing God's will? Explain your response.

_____

_____

_____

THINK ABOUT THE FUTURE

Maybe you've never given much thought to your *full* potential. You might have considered your professional abilities, aptitude for parenting, or financial prospects, but never your *full* potential. Why? It is easy to limit our future based on accomplishments or failures of the past. If we embrace that attitude, it simply means that we cannot see ourselves as anything more than what we've already been. The Israelites were that way. For forty years they wandered in the desert aware of the Promised Land but unable to enter into it. At the end of the book of Deuteronomy, Moses died.

Read **Joshua 1:1–9**. The Israelites were at a crossroad. They could either continue as wanderers or embrace their destiny. You are at a similar crossroad right now. You can move forward with God or remain as you've always been. It's your choice.

Review **Joshua 1:6–9.**

1. What did God say to Joshua three times?

_____

_____

2. As you consider your future, what advice can you glean from these verses?

_____

_____

3. Where should you find strength and courage to pursue your full potential?

_____

_____

4. Write a prayer asking God to help you identify His plans for your life. Ask Him to help you eliminate any distractions so that your life becomes all He intends it to be.

_____

_____

_____

_____

Don't Settle for Less

Read Chapter 2 of *How to Reach Your Full Potential for God*

Scripture Passage: Psalm 139:13–16

THINK ABOUT TODAY

Not everyone shares the same approach to life. Some people seize every moment and lead extraordinary lives, while others seem ambivalent about their own existence and simply get by. One's outlook is dependent upon one's attitude toward God. And because He created us, the Lord knows best how we should live.

1. Consider the following views of life and describe the attitude toward God each accompanies. There are no right or wrong answers.

a. I am excited about my life.

_____

_____

b. I am merely existing.

_____

_____

c. I am moving with confidence toward a desirable goal.

_____

_____

d. I am drifting along from day to day without any sense of purpose or direction.

_____

_____

2. What brings real joy to your life?

_____

_____

3. What is the eternal significance of your answer(s) above?

_____

_____

4. Based on your previous responses, how elusive is authentic joy?

___ easy to find

___ found only in fleeting moments

___ can't be found

5. Who did God create you to be, and what does He intend for you to do?

_____

_____

6. Many people have lost hope and consequently are bored. Why? Because they are not "actively, intentionally, and purposefully pursuing what God has planned and desired for them" (p. 8). Place an X on the line below indicating the amount of effort you give to working toward God's purpose for your life.

I'm in "park"   I'm in "neutral"   Moving with traffic   Accelerating

_____

THINK ABOUT GOD

"If you truly want to pursue and reach your full potential, then you must face up to these two truths:

Truth #1: God has placed more within you than you realize.
Truth #2: You likely have settled for the life you have at present" (p. 8).

1. Spend a few moments considering the truths above. What is your initial response to each one?

Truth #1:

_____

_____

Truth #2:

_____

_____

2. At one time, children received grades of *O* (outstanding), *S* (satisfactory), and *U* (unsatisfactory). If your relationship with God today were graded using this scale, what mark would you receive and why?

_____

_____

_____

3. "If a person becomes content with what is average, minimally acceptable, or satisfactory, she will rarely exert the effort or hold out the hope of something that is truly exemplary, outstanding, or superlative" (pp. 8–9). Which words best describe how you perceive your life?

___ below average, unacceptable, dissatisfying

___ average, acceptable, satisfactory

___ exemplary, outstanding, superlative

4. What is the correlation between your expectations and achievements?

___ I achieve more than I expect.

___ I achieve what I expect.

___ I achieve less than I expect.

5. What would be the end result of raising your expectations and pursuing a life that is "exemplary, outstanding, and superlative"?

_____

_____

_____

6. Read **Psalm 139:13–16**. How does God see you?

_____

_____

_____

7. Complete the following statements:

a. Because I am fearfully and wonderfully made, I will

_____

_____

b. Because the Lord knows everything about me, I will

_____

_____

c. Because God is the Author and Finisher of my days, I will

_____

_____

THINK ABOUT THE FUTURE

God has a plan for you and your future, and He wants you to know it. He has provided the tools and resources to uncover and embrace His plan. But there are plenty of distractions to cloud your vision and keep you too busy to hear the Lord's voice.

Go back and take another look at **Psalm 139:13–16**. Our society generally disagrees with the psalmist, and its values permeate every aspect of culture. Yet God's truth as revealed in Scripture transcends all of the world's philosophies. As believers, we must protect our self-understanding from conflicting viewpoints. Take a closer look at the "Five Key Principles about Your Potential" (p. 16) and let them guide your thoughts about the future.

1. After you've reread the **Five Key Principles about Your Potential** (p. 16) respond to the following questions:

    a. In your opinion, what percentage of your full potential have you already achieved?

    0 ——— 20 ——— 40 ——— 60 ——— 80 ——— 100

    b. If God asked, "How are you bringing glory to Me through your life?" what would be your response?

    _____

    _____

    _____

    c. Reflect on your achievements so far. How much of reaching your potential has been due to your efforts, desires, and strength?

    _____

    _____

    _____

d. Is your relationship with the Lord taking you to the next level? Why or why not?

_____

_____

_____

e. "God has also created you with the desires, dreams, and disposition to *become* a person with whom He enjoys fellowship and spiritual intimacy." Is there anything in your life that hinders fellowship and spiritual intimacy with the Father? If so, what should you do about it?

_____

_____

_____

f. How can you go beyond personal limitations and into the fullness of God's plan for your life?

_____

_____

_____

2. What is the role of the following in achieving your God-given potential? Check any that apply.

- personal Bible study and prayer
- worship
- small group Bible study
- accountability with other believers
- entertainment and socializing

3. Review the section of chapter two entitled "Your Potential Includes Both Attributes and Abilities." What is the difference between *attributes* and *abilities*?

_____

_____

_____

List some of your attributes and abilities in the space provided below.

Attributes   *Abilities*

_____

_____

_____

_____

4. How does the prospect of pursuing your full potential make you feel?

_____

_____

_____

5. "Many people live at the level of good. As a result, they miss the level of best" (p. 24). Is this statement true about you? If so, what changes will you make to your life and attitude? If not, how will you guard against adopting the world's view of your potential?

_____

_____

_____

_____

_____

6. What are three specific things you need to do to let God control your life? Make this request part of your daily prayer time with God.

_____

_____

_____

_____

_____

READY . . . SET . . . PURSUE YOUR POTENTIAL!

Read Chapter 3 of *How to Reach Your Full Potential for God*

Scripture Passage: John 21:1–14

THINK ABOUT TODAY

It is one thing to have potential, but it's another to pursue it. Perhaps you are waiting for something to launch you on the path to fulfillment. Maybe you have put your pursuit of God's best on hold, believing other needs are more pressing. Whatever your situation, the truth is that you must make a decision: chase after your potential or miss out on who God intends you to be.

1. Complete the following statement: I will begin pursuing my full potential when . . .

2. Which of the following most limits you?
   __ I make up excuses.
   __ I have exempted myself from the pursuit of my full potential.
   __ I condemn myself for waiting or procrastinating.

3. What should you do about the "shackles" that hinder your growth?
   __ Keep doing what I'm doing.
   __ Look for a new shackle.
   __ Throw off the shackles and pursue God's plan for my life.

4. "What you have done in the past does not dictate what God is still able to do in you and through you in the future!" (p. 26). What is your initial reaction to this statement?

   _____

   _____

   _____

5. Read the statement above again. If a stranger were to watch your life for 24 hours, would he or she conclude that this is true of you? Why or why not?

   _____

   _____

   _____

6. As you consider pursuing your full potential, what are some of the obstacles you must face?

_____

_____

_____

7. What is the role of faith in overcoming these challenges?

_____

_____

_____

THINK ABOUT GOD

It's not easy to change your attitude, yet this is exactly what is required of you to begin pursuing your full potential. Often, before adults will adopt a new lifestyle, they must first be convinced that their previous approach is inadequate. But acknowledging the need to change is only the first step. Making it concrete in your life is where the greatest difficulties lie.

1. What percentage of your moment-by-moment decisions hinge upon instant gratification rather than careful consideration of long-term consequences?

0 ———— 25 ———— 50 ———— 75 ———— 100

2. Describe a time when focusing on yourself negatively affected a relationship.

_____

_____

_____

3. Which of the following questions do you ask most often?

__ What brings me immediate pleasure and satisfaction?

__ What does God have in mind for my life?

4. What influences your sense of self-worth? Check all that apply.

__ entertainment

__ relationships

__ education

__ hobbies

__ goals

__ possessions

__ employment

__ appearance

__ service

__ God

__ other: _____

5. In what areas of life are you most likely to compare yourself to others? What does that say about your relationship with and trust in God?

_____

_____

_____

_____

_____

6. Which of the following affects your full potential?

__ family

__ education

__ culture

__ finances

__ personality

__ other: _____

Based on the factors mentioned above, describe someone you know who achieved far more than seemed possible.

_____

_____

_____

What keeps this from happening in your life?

_____

_____

_____

7. "People with a fear of disappointment are often perfectionists who expect too much too soon—both from themselves and from other people" (p. 34). Are you afraid of disappointing yourself or someone else?

_____

_____

_____

Why is disappointing others a big deal?

_____

_____

_____

8. Would you rather try and risk failing or do nothing and make zero progress? Explain your response.

_____

_____

_____

Throughout the Bible we see the Lord use a person's failure to bring about great, God-honoring results. Describe a time when God used your failure to bring about something great.

_____

_____

_____

9. Consider the hurdle of laziness and respond to the following questions as they relate to fulfilling the Lord's plan for your life.

a. Are you striving to reach your potential by making the most of every day?

_____

_____

_____

b. Do you perform your duties in a slipshod manner, or do you give every task your best effort?

_____

_____

_____

c. Is your schedule balanced?

_____

_____

_____

d. Have you determined what impact or influence the Father desires you to have? If so, explain.

_____

_____

_____

THINK ABOUT THE FUTURE

It is easy to doubt our value and consider ourselves unfit to serve the Lord. But we see throughout Scripture examples of God using sinful people who were willing to let Him rule their lives.

Apart from Jesus, there are no perfect people in Scripture. Yet many believers remain paralyzed by fear or unwilling to be used by God. Others are concerned with interests of no eternal value, not what matters to the Lord. Ask any pastor who has tried to recruit volunteers. He will tell you the most common response of would-be helpers is, "I'm just not good at that." But on the other side of that excuse is a striking truth: "You cannot reach your potential in your own strength and ability" (p. 38).

1. Review **John 21:1–14**. Name some tasks the disciples were good at doing.

_____

_____

_____

2. How might God use your skills and abilities in and through your church?

_____

_____

_____

3. What are some things God wants you to do that are outside of your current abilities?

_____

_____

_____

4. List three things you will do in response to this lesson.

_____

_____

_____

Essential #1
A Clean Heart

Read Chapter 4 of *How to Reach Your Full Potential for God*

Scripture Passage: Psalm 139:23–24

THINK ABOUT TODAY

Health professionals constantly remind us about the importance of washing our hands to prevent the spread of germs. And many people are employed in cleaning-related businesses or industries. Wouldn't you agree that cleanliness is important to our lives? Our relationship with God is no exception.

1. Use the space provided (and additional paper if needed) to describe how you came to know Jesus Christ as your Lord and Savior.

---

2. If you died and God asked you to explain why He should let you into heaven, what would you say?

---

3. The first essential necessary to pursuing your God-given potential is a clean heart. Based on what you read in chapter four, how would you describe a clean heart?

---

4. "You were born with a bent away from God. That is true for every person. Every person is born with a sinful nature. We

are born with a focus on self and on self-gratification" (p. 39). This statement refers to the way you were when you were born. Where are you on the following scale?

Focused on self ———————————— Focused on God

5. Why is it so important for believers to continually refocus on God and His desires for them?

_____

_____

_____

_____

_____

How do you accomplish this in your life?

_____

_____

_____

THINK ABOUT GOD

We are estranged from God. No amount of good behavior or church-going will fix that. Our relationship with Him is broken and justifiably so. We know what He expects of us and yet do as we please, choosing to sin rather than obey Him. The Lord has every right to reject us. So, why does He love us so much?

1. In what ways do some people attempt to fix their relationship with God?

_____

_____

_____

2. Think about your life. Have you ever done something good in order to earn the Father's love or favor? Why or why not?

_____

_____

_____

_____

_____

3. Reflect on your spiritual growth from the point of your salvation until now. In what way(s) have you . . .

   a. been renewed in your mind?

   b. been redirected to walk God's path?

   c. refocused your desires?

   d. been reenergized to fulfill God's purposes?

4. "The Holy Spirit—the promise of the Father and the gift to every person who believes in Christ Jesus as the Son of God—unfolds before us all that the Father has made us to be and to do" (p. 41). When you consider your potential, is it based more on what the Holy Spirit has revealed or on what you have imagined possible? Explain your response.

_____

_____

_____

_____

_____

5. The Holy Spirit will not help us do anything outside of God's plan and purpose for our lives. How should this truth affect the way you pray for the Lord's help and assistance?

_____

_____

_____

_____

_____

6. What is your definition of sin?

_____

_____

_____

How does sin affect your relationship with Jesus Christ?

_____

_____

_____

_____

_____

7. Read **Psalm 139:23–24**. What part of your life is invisible to God?

How often should your prayer echo the psalmist's?

__ every moment

__ at the end of each day

__ only when I've thought or done something really bad

__ never, because my sins are forgiven; I can do what I want

THINK ABOUT THE FUTURE

The psalmist wanted to be reminded of anything he needed to confess. He knew that his sin put a barrier between him and God. Even though he was forgiven, with unconfessed sin, his life lacked meaning, purpose, and intimacy with the Father. This is where it gets personal for us. We must understand the natural consequences of disobedience and how seemingly insignificant choices affect our lives.

In Matthew 5:8, Jesus said, "Blessed are the pure in heart, for they shall see God." This was a reference to our daily, ongoing ability to see the Lord at work in our lives. We must pause for a moment, however, and consider the other side of Jesus' statement. People with an impure heart cannot see God or His work in their lives.

1. Think about your life. If seeing God's plan and purpose is a byproduct of personal purity, how pure (in His eyes) is your life?

_____

_____

_____

2. Do you expect the Lord to reveal your full potential if you don't live by His principles and rules? Why or why not?

_____

_____

_____

3. Based on what you read in chapter four, is purity possible for today's Christian? Explain your response.

_____

_____

_____

4. Proverbs 4:23 tells us to "keep" our hearts. What does this mean and how are we supposed to do it?

_____

_____

_____

The Bible describes itself as a light on your path. That, of course, assumes you've chosen to follow God's will for your life. It is ridiculous to expect Him to illumine a route that takes you away from Him and His purposes.

This is why personal Bible study is so important. It redirects our steps to help us keep walking with the Lord. Every situation or decision you face is addressed specifically or in principle within the pages of Scripture. God hasn't hidden His desires—He has given them to us in bound copies. Why, then, are so many believers clueless about God's plan for their lives?

5. Read Psalm 119:11–15. Is this passage true about you? If so, how? If not, why?

_____

_____

_____

6. In John 14:15, Jesus said, "If you love Me, you will keep My commandments." We can turn that verse around and say, "If

I'm keeping God's commandments, I love Him." But *keeping* means more than mindless obedience. It means we have internalized the instruction and it is characteristic of our lives. When people meet you for the first time, what do you think they believe is most important to you?

_____

_____

_____

How should you live this week so that "God" is the answer to the question above?

_____

_____

_____

What lifestyle changes can you make to eliminate any confusion about your priorities?

_____

_____

_____

ESSENTIAL #2
A CLEAR MIND

Read Chapter 5 of *How to Reach Your Full Potential for God*

Scripture Passage: James 1:5–8

THINK ABOUT TODAY

Many believers don't realize just how passive they are. Sure, we choose to engage with passion in a lot of different activities and causes, but are we really passionate about discovering and living out God's plan and purpose for our lives?

1. Read the following statements and place a number by each one indicating its truthfulness to your life. Use the following scale:

0 = not true at all / 1 = sometimes true / 2 = always true

__ I am a passive person, accepting whatever is handed me.

__ I sit back, disengaged from the world as it passes me by.

__ I am seeking to do my best in every area of life.

__ I have an insatiable hunger to know what God will do in and through me.

__ I have a passion for self-discovery—to test my limits and see what I can accomplish.

__ I desire to discover and explore my gifts and talents.

Reflect on your responses above and decide if the following statement is true or false:

I am a passive Christian. True / False

2. What is the difference between being interested in spirituality and having an intimate relationship with God?

_____

_____

_____

3. Consider your daily activities and use the following phrases to complete the statement below. Use each word or phrase only once.

- God
- the world

I view _____ through _____'s eyes.

4. When you make decisions in the following areas, are you more likely to seek advice from society or God?

   a. morality

   b. finances

   c. relationships

   d. entertainment

THINK ABOUT GOD

"We cannot educate ourselves to have Christ's mind. In other words, we cannot go to a particular school and take a particular course or series of courses and emerge with a degree that gives us the initials M.C. (Mind of Christ) after our names. Nevertheless, we can have the mind of Christ if we are willing to receive what God desires to give us" (p. 58).

1. There are three characteristics of a person who has the mind of Christ. The first is a perspective of *wholeness*. Describe how your relationship with God affects the whole of your life.

   _____

   _____

   _____

2. Read **Proverbs 23:7**. What does this verse say about the connection of our thoughts to other areas of life?

   _____

   _____

   _____

3. Every facet of our lives is connected to the others, whether we realize it or not. Is your relationship with God confined to church attendance, or does it permeate the rest of your life, every day, all week long? Explain your response.

_____

_____

_____

4. "Happiness is a cheap and temporary substitute for the real joy that comes from having a solid relationship with God. Happiness is fleeting and based on outer circumstances. Joy is lasting and rooted deeply in the spirit" (p. 61). Which is your life's aim—happiness or joy? Explain your response.

_____

_____

_____

5. The second characteristic of a person with the mind of Christ is *focus* rather than *fragmentation*. Describe your approach to multitasking throughout the day.

_____

_____

_____

When you multitask, you are really expressing the importance of momentary distractions. For instance, you might choose to focus on a conversation while driving rather than safely operating your car. Or maybe you choose to surf the Internet rather than complete your work. In a similar way, we can be distracted from our pursuit of God. How about you? Does anything take priority over your relationship with Christ? If so, explain.

_____

_____

_____

6. The third characteristic of a person with Christ's mind is *creativity*. Describe how God's creativity is made visible through your life.

_____

_____

_____

7. There are two ways to view conversion. Which one best represents your point of view? Finish this sentence: When I received Christ . . .

___ I asked Him to come into my life.

___ I asked Him to live through me.

What is the difference between these two statements?

_____

_____

8. When it comes to studying God's Word, do you pursue intelligence or wisdom?

_____

_____

_____

What is the difference between intelligence and wisdom?

_____

_____

_____

9. Read **James 1:5–8** and then write that passage in your own words.

_____

_____

_____

_____

_____

10. How can you keep from doubting God? What is the role of daily, personal Bible study and prayer in this process?

_____

_____

_____

THINK ABOUT THE FUTURE

1. What does "double-minded" mean?

_____

_____

_____

In what areas of life do you sometimes exhibit double-mindedness?

_____

_____

_____

2. Finish this sentence: I determine right and wrong by choosing what . . .

__ brings the greatest pleasure to my life.

__ works to my advantage.

__ goes with the flow of my relationships.

__ God says.

3. When you think about the way in which you "feed" your mind, of what does your mental diet consist?

__ unhealthy snacks

__ junk food

__ healthy meals

__ a little bit of everything

4. Think about the things you put in your mind. As you plan what you will do tonight, consider the following questions:

Does this enhance my spiritual life?
Yes / No

Does this promote my overall well-being and wholeness?
Yes / No

Does this uplift me, edify me, or inspire me to greater good?
Yes / No

Does this lead to holiness?

Yes / No

Does this increase the work of God in my life?

Yes / No

Does this add to my ability to discern good from evil, right from wrong, and to determine what is best?

Yes / No

Based on these questions, should you proceed with your plans? Why or why not?

_____

_____

_____

5. Read **Philippians 2:5–8** and describe your strategy for acquiring a clear mind. Read pages 79–83 for insight into this process.

_____

_____

_____

6. Read and memorize **Romans 12:2**. What is God telling you to do through this verse?

_____

_____

_____

ESSENTIAL #3
USING YOUR GIFTS

Read Chapter 6 of *How to Reach Your Full Potential for God*

Scripture Passage: Exodus 35:31–35

THINK ABOUT TODAY

We all like gifts. Many of us enjoy giving them, and most of us enjoy receiving them. It should come as no surprise that God, the greatest Giver of all, endows us with talents and abilities to fulfill His purpose for our lives. In and through Him, we have all we need to do everything the Lord wills. Corporately, our giftedness enables the church to fulfill its mission.

1. What are some things you are passionate about doing and can accomplish without much difficulty?

_____

_____

_____

2. What are you typically doing when you are most useful to God?

_____

_____

_____

3. When you consider your talents and gifts, are they primarily used for your personal benefit or God's glory? Explain your response.

_____

_____

_____

4. As you think about this lesson, what do you want to know about your spiritual gifts?

_____

_____

_____

When you discover your spiritual gifts, what do you plan to do with them?

__ Use them to make a living.

__ Use them to make myself famous.

__ Use them through the church to glorify God.

__ Nothing. I'm just curious.

5. "Knowing your God-given gifts and talents is vital to your potential. It is never enough just to enjoy something or to hope that you can develop a gift you do not have" (p. 96). How are your gifts connected to your potential?

_____

_____

_____

As you pursue your potential, why is knowing your gifts so important?

_____

_____

_____

THINK ABOUT GOD

Some of us have natural abilities that have been present since birth. These are given by God, but they are not spiritual gifts. The latter come to us through the Holy Spirit at the point of our salvation.

1. Review the information under the heading "Your Gifts from Birth" (pp. 96–102) and list three gifts that are evident in your daily activities. Also, describe how each manifests in your life.

Gift	*How It Is Used*
1. _____	
2. _____	
3. _____	

2. Review the list above and identify some ways these gifts could be used in service to God and ministry to others.

_____

_____

_____

3. Recap your life story, paying particular attention to where you lived and how each situation influenced you (please use a separate sheet of paper).

4. "Nobody else on earth, not even those of your generation who grew up in the area where you were born and raised, has precisely your context of time and space" (p. 102). List some things your life experiences have prepared you to do.

_____

_____

_____

_____

_____

5. "Write down what you actually recognize as factors that have been built into your life from your birth. Do not list gifts that you think would be what other people would want you to have. List what is. Construct a profile of your authentic, true

self" (p. 103). Use a separate piece of paper or a personal jour-nal to complete this task. Be honest with yourself about who you are and who you believe God intends you to be.

6. Read **Exodus 35:31–35**. Write a passage similar to this with you as the subject. Include specific ways you have been equipped to pursue your God-given potential.

_____

_____

_____

_____

_____

_____

_____

THINK ABOUT THE FUTURE

What would happen if one of today's top athletes quit working out, practic-ing, and monitoring his nutrition? It wouldn't take long for that person to lose his ability to compete. Successful athletes recognize the importance of a consistent training regimen. We would do well to adopt their discipline, not physically, but spiritually. Our natural inclination is to neglect spiri-tual growth. If we don't make it a priority, we will become little more than lazy people who once had great potential.

1. "*Teaching* is the impartation of concepts, facts, principles, and general information" (p. 105). Why is it important to have a good role model, mentor, or coach?

_____

_____

_____

List some people in your life who fit the criteria of a role model, mentor, or coach.

_____

_____

_____

2. Trainers motivate you to keep practicing something until you acquire the skill. For what are you in "training" and who is your trainer?

_____

_____

_____

3. "[T]he best things you can study fall within the realm of your natural gifts. That is where you will find your greatest satisfaction and success" (p. 106). What are you studying?

_____

_____

_____

How does your chosen subject connect to your natural gifts?

___ no connection

___ loose connection

___ strong connection

4. "God did not give you your gifts to have you squander them, ignore them, or dabble at them. He gave them to you so you might develop them to the highest levels possible" (p. 107). When it comes to developing your gifts, where are you? Place an X on the line indicating your present level of development.

ignoring my gifts ⟵—————————⟶ in daily training

Explain your response.

_____

_____

_____

5. List below three of your strengths and three of your weaknesses.

My strengths:

1. _____

2. _____

3. _____

My weaknesses:

1. _____

2. _____

3. _____

6. Review the information about ministry-related gifts on pages 113–4. In light of your strengths and weaknesses, which ministry-related gifts are possibilities for you?

7. Take a look at the chart on page 114. List the two gifts that, based on their expression, are most evident in your life.

_____

_____

_____

8. The most perfect example of giftedness in action was the life of Jesus. When you consider the two gifts listed above, how can you be more like Him in using them?

_____

_____

_____

9. What do the following passages say about using your gifts, in harmony with other believers, through your church?

• John 15:12

_____

_____

• Romans 12:10

_____

_____

• Ephesians 4:1–3

_____

_____

- Colossians 3:15

_____

_____

Essential #4
A Healthy Body

Read Chapter 7 of *How to Reach Your Full Potential for God*

Scripture Passage: 1 Corinthians 6:12–14, 19–20

THINK ABOUT TODAY

"A healthy body is critical to your preparation and execution of the various activities and ministry opportunities that God gives you. You *need* a healthy body to fulfill your eternal destiny and achieve the success God has designed for you" (p. 126). The pursuit of reaching your potential can be stalled or prevented if you aren't physically healthy.

1. Rate your strength in the following areas, 1 being "Poor" and 5 being "Excellent."

    a. concentration   1 2 3 4 5

    b. enthusiasm   1 2 3 4 5

    c. clear thinking   1 2 3 4 5

    d. motivation   1 2 3 4 5

    e. perseverance   1 2 3 4 5

    f. timeliness   1 2 3 4 5

2. How does your physical condition affect your pursuit of God's best?

    _____

    _____

    _____

3. Consider your current habits in caring for yourself physically. If you continue on your present path, how healthy will you be in five or ten years?

    __ I will be healthier than I am today.

    __ I will be as healthy as I am today.

    __ I will be in worse shape than I am today.

    Are you satisfied with your response?

    __ **Yes.** How can you encourage others to pursue physical health?

    __ **No.** What will you do about it and when will you start?

4. What are three things you do to improve your health?

_____

_____

_____

Name three things you do that worsen your health.

_____

_____

_____

THINK ABOUT GOD

The Bible was written at a time when things were much different. Children weren't prone to spending countless hours in front of a television or playing video games. And many of the social pastimes common today were not yet in existence. Therefore, Scripture doesn't speak specifically to many activities we might question. This leaves many believers thinking that anything goes. The fact is, however, that the Bible *does* speak specifically or in principle to every situation we face.

1. Read **1 Corinthians 6:12–14, 19–20.** "The real issue was whether a person was acting in a way that built up another's faith or paved the way for an unbeliever to receive Jesus Christ as his personal Savior" (p. 130). Based on this passage, what should be a Christian's main concern—personal preference or spiritual influence? Explain your response.

_____

_____

_____

2. Review the passage above and the information on pages 130–2. How should the principles affect your attitude and behaviors? Be specific.

a. Because the body is the temple of the Holy Spirit . . .

I will stop

_____

_____

_____

I will start

_____

_____

_____

b. Because I am instructed to glorify God in my body . . .

I will stop

_____

_____

_____

I will start

_____

_____

_____

3. Should believers have the freedom to engage in any activity they want as long as it doesn't affect other people? Explain your response using the Bible.

_____

_____

_____

4. What is the difference between ownership and stewardship?

_____

_____

_____

When it comes to your body, are you the owner or the steward? Explain your response.

_____

_____

_____

5. "If you allow your body to become sluggish, polluted, weak, or infected when you have the ability to keep it active, cleansed, strong, and protected, you will miss out on exciting, worthy, and potential-fulfilling opportunities to serve others and bring glory to God" (p. 136). What are some potential-fulfilling opportunities you are missing because you are not glorifying God in your body?

_____

_____

_____

6. See pages 137–8. How do you keep your body . . .

a. clean?

_____

_____

b. fully functioning?

_____

_____

c. strong?

_____

_____

d. healthy?

_____

_____

THINK ABOUT THE FUTURE

We can't stop unpleasant things from happening in life. Everyone goes through hard times regardless of our relationship with the Lord and how we care for our bodies. Godly people die of terminal illnesses while the wicked seem to thrive. Why? We don't know the answer to that question. But we do know that God works through us and our circumstances to reveal Himself to a doubting, hurting world.

God has given us our bodies. We should do our part, while we can, to keep them in top operating condition. This means avoiding harmful habits and activities, including alcohol and tobacco consumption, but also poor sleep patterns and lack of exercise.

1. Think back over the past 24–48 hours and list all of the foods and beverages you have consumed.

_____

_____

_____

2. Review the list above and place a "+" by anything you believe to be nutritious and beneficial. Place a "–" by harmful items or those that lack nutritional benefit. Count the positives and subtract the negatives. Based on your habits, have you strengthened or weakened your body through the things you consumed? Explain your response.

_____

_____

_____

3. Now think about your physical activity over the past 24–48 hours. List the amount of time you spent exercising. How would you rate your fitness habits?

__ I'm a couch potato.

__ I exercise when I have time.

__ I intend to start exercising soon.

__ Exercise is a part of my everyday routine.

4. Mark the actions on the following list that you need to incorporate into your life:

__ practice good nutrition

__ begin an exercise program

__ learn more about medications I am prescribed

__ get medical advice on supplements and over-the-counter drugs

__ routinely monitor my blood pressure, cholesterol, weight, etc.

__ get a second opinion for any recommended surgeries or procedures

__ take responsibility for my health

__ stop harmful habits and be willing to get professional help if needed

__ practice prevention now rather than seek a cure in the future

5. Which of the following enemies are you allowing into your body? See pages 146–9.

__ Alcohol

__ Tobacco

__ Drugs

__ Sexually transmitted diseases

The Bible clearly teaches that sex outside of marriage is a sin. Sin has consequences. Why would you willingly engage in activity that is forbidden by God?

_____

_____

_____

If you consume alcohol, tobacco, and drugs, but can't quit, you are addicted and need assistance. Don't hesitate to get help. Call someone today.

6. Another enemy of a healthy lifestyle is stress. Which of the following symptoms are you experiencing?

__ hatred

__ bitterness

__ anger

__ resentment

__ worry, anxiety, and frustration

__ discouragement, low self-value or low self-worth

__ grief

__ failure

__ overindulgence in any area of life, including overwork and overeating

__ loss, including loss of a job, relationship, or loved one

7. Check your attitude about your health by responding to these questions:

• How do you feel about your body?

_____

_____

• How do you feel about caring for your body, including exercise?

_____

_____

- What is your attitude toward health?

_____

_____

- How do feel about God's ownership of your body?

_____

_____

- What is your attitude toward good nutrition?

_____

_____

8. What will you do in response to this lesson?

_____

_____

_____

_____

_____

ESSENTIAL #5
RIGHT RELATIONSHIPS

Read Chapter 8 of *How to Reach Your Full Potential for God*

Scripture Passage: *Acts 13:1–5*

THINK ABOUT TODAY

"Our relationships determine to a great extent whether we succeed at our tasks. They determine our degree of joy as we pursue various goals and engage in various activities. Our relationships determine the degree to which we successfully overcome adversities and hardships" (p. 157).

1. Describe a time when facing adversity or hardship was made easier because of one or more relationships.

_____

_____

_____

2. Name five people you influence most and the five people who most influence you:

        I influence: I am influenced by:

1. _____   _____

2. _____   _____

3. _____   _____

4. _____   _____

5. _____   _____

3. Think about the quality of your relationships. Grade yourself on an A to F scale in response to the following statements, "A" meaning excellent and "F" failing.

___ I have friends I can count on in times of trouble.

___ I know I am loved, appreciated, and valued by my friends.

___ I have healthy give-and-take relationships.

___ My primary relationships are spiritually beneficial to everyone involved.

___ My relationships facilitate or encourage the pursuit of my full potential.

4. Describe the kind of friend you are to the people with whom you are closest.

_____

_____

_____

5. Think about your main relationships.

___ I am a better friend to others than they are to me.

___ I treat my friends equally to how they treat me.

___ I expect more from others than I'm willing to give in return.

THINK ABOUT GOD

"All of the previous topics we have covered—a clean heart, a clear mind, a set of talents and gifts, and a healthy body—are related to the way you interact with other people. The lives of other people, in turn, impact your understanding of what it means to live in a forgiven, intimate, pure relationship with God and others, what it means to have a clear mind, what it means to have and use your natural and ministry-motivated gifts, and what it means to live in as much health and vitality as you can" (p.157).

1. Read **Acts 13:1–5**. The early church sent people out in teams to do ministry. If your church sent you into ministry, with whom would you be partnered and why?

_____

_____

_____

2. There are four basic truths about relationships. Review these on pages 160–1, and then read the statements below. Mark the one in each pair that is most true about you and how you relate to others.

___ 1a. My key relationships are spiritually beneficial to everyone involved.

___ 1b. Spiritual matters are not a part of my key relationships.

___ 2a. My friends know they can count on me in times of need.

___ 2b. I value my relationships because of their benefit to me.

___ 3a. I have well-defined boundaries for my relationships.

___ 3b. I am willing to tolerate any behavior in order to have friends.

___ 4a. My relationships are characterized by honesty and forgiveness.

___ 4b. My friends are disposable. When I get what I want, I'm finished.

3. What are three things you can do to improve the spiritual quality of your interactions with friends and family?

a. _____

b. _____

c. _____

4. "As problematic as the overall matter of relationships can be, relationships are God's plan for us. God does not want anyone to be a lone ranger or to attempt to live as an isolated unit totally independent from all other people. We become who we are, we develop our character, and we are enriched and prepared for various tasks and experiences as we are in relationship with others" (pp. 163–4). How is your character affected by your current relationships?

_____

_____

_____

5. You can have neutral connections with acquaintances, but there's no middle ground in meaningful relationships: they are either beneficial or detrimental. Describe your most helpful relationship. What makes it different from the others?

_____

_____

_____

Now describe the relationship that is most detrimental.

_____

_____

_____

6. Take a moment to ask God for His counsel in dealing with the harmful relationships in your life. When He reveals to you what to do, write it down and share your plans with a trustworthy friend, mentor, or pastor. Ask the person you tell to hold you accountable.

_____

_____

_____

_____

_____

_____

_____

_____

THINK ABOUT THE FUTURE

"Some people do not seem to think that it is necessary or even possible to make conscious choices about who they will have in their lives. My contention is that God wants you to have an active role in choosing the people in your life and, if you are a parent, choosing the people in your children's lives" (p. 165).

1. You most likely have several meaningful relationships. Consider one of them as you complete the following activity. Later, you will want to evaluate all of your relationships using this method.

   Using the numbers 1, 2, and 3 to indicate "never," "sometimes," and "always" (respectively), please respond to the following sentence, beginning with "My friend."

a. builds my confidence	1	2	3
b. encourages me when I am discouraged	1	2	3
c. motivates me to do my best	1	2	3
d. stimulates my creativity	1	2	3
e. energizes me	1	2	3
f. comforts me when I am hurting	1	2	3
g. defends me when I am criticized	1	2	3
h. forgives my mistakes	1	2	3
i. loves me unconditionally	1	2	3
j. accepts me as I am	1	2	3
k. confronts me when I am wrong	1	2	3
l. anticipates my needs	1	2	3

Now total the points represented by the numbers circled. The maximum score is 36 and the minimum is 12.

My relationship with _____ scored _____ out of 36. Based on your score, is your relationship . . .

__ weak (12–18 points)

__ average (19–30 points)

__ excellent (31–36 points)

2. Now consider one of your weaker or less spiritually beneficial relationships. Which of the following statements are true of that relationship? Mark all that apply.

__ It dims my vision.

__ It discourages me from pursuing my God-given potential.

__ It drags me down emotionally.

__ It derails me from doing things I know I should do.

__ It defeats me at every turn.

__ It destroys my career, ministry, or physical well-being.

What would God have you do about relationships that exhibit one or more of the characteristics above? See pages 169–70.

__ Pray for the person to change.

__ Give up on pursuing my God-given potential.

__ Sever the relationship.

__ Grow in my relationship with God in spite of this friendship.

__ Other: _____

3. How do you choose people with whom you want a relationship? What are the characteristics you seek? Review pages 172–3 for a list of suggested questions to ask about potential friends.

ESSENTIAL #6
A BALANCED SCHEDULE

Read Chapter 9 of *How to Reach Your Full Potential for God*

Scripture Passages: Psalm 100:4; Matthew 6:33; Mark 6:30–32; Luke 10:38–42; John 15:13; 1 Corinthians 6:19; Hebrews 10:24–25

THINK ABOUT TODAY

"I believe we are wise to conclude that while our days are numbered by the Lord, He gives us tremendous freedom of choice in how we will spend our days. We are, to a great extent, responsible for living in a way that brings genuine quality to our lives" (p. 177).

1. By what criteria do you evaluate "quality of life"?

_____

_____

_____

2. What is the correlation between your spiritual health and over-all well-being?

_____

_____

_____

3. "If you are going to make the most of your life and the oppor-tunities God places before you, you must value the time that God has given you and then seek to infuse it with those things that are of highest value" (p. 180). Based on your use of time and the things in which you are interested, what activities or pursuits do you value most highly? List the top three.

   a. _____

   b. _____

   c. _____

   Does anything on the list above hinder your relationship with God? If yes, how can you reorder your priorities? If no, how can you maintain your focus?

_____

_____

_____

4. Do you manage your schedule or does it manage you? Explain what you mean.

_____

_____

_____

5. Name three passions or interests that affect your free time. Are these activities more or less important than your spiritual growth? Explain your response.

_____

_____

_____

THINK ABOUT GOD

"You are called to be a steward of your time. God has given you time to live out His purpose. To waste time is to be a poor steward. It is to fail—minute by minute, hour by hour—to do all that God purposed for you from the moment of your creation" (p. 182).

1. God gives us the days, months, and years of our lives to freely invest as we choose. On average, what percentage of your time each day do you give to serving God and knowing Him better? Place an X on the line below.

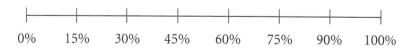

0%   15%   30%   45%   60%   75%   90%   100%

2. What typically throws your life out of balance?

_____

_____

_____

3. We can learn a lot about maintaining balance by studying Jesus'
   life. "Jesus had a public ministry, but He also had private times
   with His closest friends and associates, and He had intensely
   personal times when He was alone with His heavenly Father"
   (p. 184). Describe your:

   a. public ministry:

_____

_____

_____

   b. time with friends:

_____

_____

_____

   c. time alone with God:

_____

_____

_____

4. Read **Psalm 100:4.** What is the proper beginning of prayer?

_____

_____

5. Read **Matthew 6:33**. What should be your life's chief aim?

_____

_____

6. Read **John 15:13**. How should you think about and act toward your friends?

_____

_____

_____

7. Work is important but it should be kept in perspective. What should be your attitude toward labor?

_____

_____

_____

How can you prevent becoming a workaholic?

_____

_____

_____

8. On a scale of 1 to 10, with 10 being maximum, how important to you is daily worship? _____

Read **Hebrews 10:24–25**. What does this passage say about spending time in worship with other believers?

_____

_____

_____

9. Review the account of Mary and Martha in **Luke 10:38–42**. What is the point of this story?

_____

_____

_____

10. Jesus relaxed and rested. Read **Mark 6:30–32**. What are your rest and relaxation habits?

_____

_____

_____

11. "Sleep is not an option. It is not a nicety of life, but a necessity. During deep, sound sleep, the mind processes all the bits of information gleaned from the day and sorts those bits in appropriate ways for recall and use" (p. 197). Are your sleep habits beneficial or harmful to your overall effectiveness for God? Explain your response.

_____

_____

_____

12. Exercise keeps us mentally, emotionally, and spiritually fit. How often do you exercise?

__ daily

__ several times per week

__ weekly

__ never

Based on **1 Corinthians 6:19**, how should you alter your exercise habits?

_____

_____

_____

THINK ABOUT THE FUTURE

"Do you talk to God . . . about your schedule? Or do you hurl yourself into an almost frantic routine each day, rushing from place to place and chore to chore, thinking that in all of your busyness you are accomplishing real work or establishing real relationships?" (p. 201).

1. Jesus' approach to life will work at any time, anywhere. Consider how you can apply the following principles to your schedule.
   a. **Never make excuses for any aspect of your schedule** (p. 201). Live without the need for the approval of others.
   b. **Never get hurried or flustered in moving from place to place** (p. 201). Let God guide you toward the encounters that are most meaningful.
   c. **Don't let your schedule become stressful.** Learn what is important and what is unimportant.

2. Review your weekly commitments by asking yourself the following questions:

   a. What do I need to do?

_____

_____

b. Which of these activities is critical to God's purpose for my life?

_____

_____

c. What should I complete?

_____

_____

d. Can I delegate anything?

_____

_____

e. What needs to be left undone?

_____

_____

It's time to take control of your schedule. See the chart on page 202 and work through the process on page 203.

3. Prioritize the following activities sequentially based on importance, beginning with "1" for most important.

___ prayer

___ time with family and friends

___ work

___ reading, studying, or discussing God's Word

___ worship

___ rest and relaxation

4. Now consider your responses to the following questions:

a. What stresses you?

_____

_____

b. Does anything make you feel hurried or rushed?

_____

_____

c. What are you doing to meet the expectations of others?

_____

_____

5. How can you better use your time to honor God and fulfill His purpose for your life?

_____

_____

_____

ESSENTIAL #7
TAKING
GOD-APPROVED RISKS

Read Chapter 10 of *How to Reach Your Full Potential for God*

Scripture Passage: Matthew 14:22–33

THINK ABOUT TODAY

"Your potential is the sum of all the possibilities that God has for your life. And the truth is that you have absolutely no way to comprehend all of the possibilities that an all-wise, all-knowing, infinite God sees. You cannot know with your finite mind and your limited perspective all that God knows" (p. 212).

1. How would you describe yourself?

    __ I'm a risk-taker.

    __ I need some assurance before trying something new.

    __ I take no risks whatsoever.

2. As you consider your God-given potential, what are some areas of life in which you need to be more of a risk-taker?

    _____

    _____

    _____

3. What best describes your attitude?

    __ I am too afraid to risk anything.

    __ I don't know which risks to take.

    __ I am taking risks but I'm not sure they are the right ones.

    __ I continue to take risks and realize more of my potential all the time.

4. Imagine your life ten years from now. Can you foresee any risks as you follow your hopes and dreams? What are they?

    _____

    _____

    _____

5. Spiritual growth is vital to the long process of reaching one's potential. What habits will you need to form in order to sustain that growth?

_____

_____

_____

THINK ABOUT GOD

"What you may regard as a risk, from your perspective, just may be the very situation that God wants to use to strengthen your faith. What you perceive to hold the potential for loss or danger, God may very well be using to make you stronger in character. What you perceive to be a chance, very possibly could be what God is going to use to take you one giant step closer to reaching your potential" (p. 214).

1. Read **Matthew 14:22–33**. Had you been in the boat, what would have been your response to seeing Jesus walk on the water?
   ___ I would have been afraid.
   ___ I would have been amazed.
   ___ I would have asked Him to let me walk on the water, too.
   ___ I would have stayed on shore in the first place.

2. What does Peter's response say about the quality of his personal relationship with Jesus?

_____

_____

_____

3. What was the overall effect of this experience on Peter's faith?
   ___ His faith was weakened.
   ___ There was no effect on his faith.
   ___ His faith was strengthened.

4. What in your life causes you to step out of the "boat"?

_____

_____

_____

5. Think back over the past few months. Has God used an amaz-
   ing experience to teach you to trust Him more? If so, describe
   that experience. If not, why?

_____

_____

_____

6. Rank the following activities according to their perceived risk.
   Give the most risky activity a "1" and work your way down the
   list sequentially.

   __ skydiving

   __ rappelling

   __ driving a race car

   __ making a career change

   __ getting married

   __ rearing children

   __ asking for a pay raise

   __ traveling abroad

   __ completing your income taxes

   Review your rankings above and try to determine the criteria
   you use to decide the degree of risk involved in an activity. List
   your criteria on the next page.

_____

_____

_____

7. "God has numerous ways to confirm that the challenge before us is His challenge" (p. 217). How do you decide which challenges are from God and which are not?

_____

_____

_____

8. Review the section entitled Characteristics of God's Challenges (pp. 217–26). Think about a challenge you are facing right now and restate the five characteristics in response to your situation.

1) _____

2) _____

3) _____

4) _____

5) _____

9. Based on your evaluation of the situation, do you believe it is a God-given challenge? Why or why not?

_____

_____

_____

THINK ABOUT THE FUTURE

In striving to achieve your potential, you will face many challenges. As you read the Bible, you will see the heroes of our faith endure trials and difficulties time and time again. Those who faced hard times with God-given confidence saw the Lord do incredible things in and through their lives. Those who walked away from challenges often missed seeing God's activity around them.

1. How can you give the Lord control of your life on a daily basis?

_____

_____

_____

2. As you consider unconditional obedience to God, what causes you the most fear?

_____

_____

_____

How should you deal with those emotions?

_____

_____

_____

3. God's truth cannot be false and the devil's lies cannot be true. Are you more affected by the devil's lies or God's truths? Explain your response.

_____

_____

_____

4. One of the greatest hindrances to moving forward with the Lord is one's past. The devil uses old sins to keep us from believing that God forgives and forgets our failures. But in Jesus Christ, we don't have to live with regret. Write a prayer in the space below thanking God for His forgiveness. Ask Him to continually remind you of His purpose for your life.

_____

_____

_____

_____

_____

THE ONGOING
PURSUIT

Read Chapter 11 of *How to Reach Your Full Potential for God*

Scripture Passage: Micah 6:8

THINK ABOUT TODAY

"God intends for you to keep learning and to keep having new godly experiences all your life. The more you fulfill your potential, the more you will have a need for input—both knowledge and wisdom from others, and experiential wisdom that comes from application" (p. 233).

1. There is no such thing as being spiritually neutral. You either move forward or backward. Consider your daily routine and

list five things in your life that are spiritually beneficial and five things that are not.

	Things that help me grow	Things that interfere with growth
1.	_____	_____
2.	_____	_____
3.	_____	_____
4.	_____	_____
5.	_____	_____

2. In what way is your spiritual growth outwardly evident? How are you serving God in and through your church?

_____

_____

_____

3. Is your spirituality integrated with the rest of your life, including work and hobbies?

__ They are completely separate.

__ They are connected when it's in my best interest.

__ They are intertwined.

Explain your answer.

_____

_____

_____

4. When seeking help or growth in a specific area of life, what is the role of self-help books and motivational entertainment in your life?

_____

_____

_____

What is the Bible's role in relationship to these books and entertainment options?

__ The books and speakers tell me what's true about the Bible.

__ The Bible tells me what's true about the books and speakers.

5. Based on your current Bible study habits, how much influence does Scripture really have in your life? Explain your response.

_____

_____

_____

THINK ABOUT GOD

"As you go through life, you are going to face countless opportunities for new memberships, new situations, new investments, new associations, new relationships, new work or career opportunities, new alliances, and new mergers. Not every opportunity is a good one. And with even greater certainty I say to you, not every opportunity is sent you by God" (p. 236).

1. How do you know if an opportunity is from God?

   Is your decision about the opportunity most often made . . .

   __before you get involved?

   __while you're involved?

   __only in retrospect?

2. Describe a situation when you realized an activity in which you were engaged probably wasn't sent by God.

   _____

   _____

   _____

   What consequences did you experience that might have been avoided had you determined God's involvement before engaging in the activity?

   _____

   _____

   _____

3. Read **Micah 6:8** and summarize the verse by filling in the blanks below:

   Love _____ and love _____.

   How can this verse help you determine the viability of an opportunity?

   _____

   _____

   _____

4. Christians often focus more on negative behavior than the good works God calls us to in Scripture. A list of prohibitions leads to situational rules, while Bible-based principles are universally applicable. Which statement best describes your daily attitude toward God's Word?

__ I can do anything the Bible doesn't specifically prohibit.

__ When I adhere to biblical principles, the gray areas disappear.

What is the danger of operating from the first option above?

_____

_____

_____

5. "You were not redeemed by Christ on the cross to become another person's slave—employee, yes, but slave, no. You were not redeemed by Christ to do the bidding of another person, giving 100 percent of your time and energy to satisfying that person's whims and longings. No. You are to help when and how you can help in godly, affirming ways. But you are to do Christ's bidding, not the bidding of man" (p. 238). Read the quote carefully. Identify the appropriate attitude toward your:

work: _____

social life: _____

family: _____

friends: _____

entertainment: _____

hobbies and interests: _____

appearance: _____

How have you been a slave to one or more of the things listed above?

6. Are the various elements of your life working together to bring glory to God? If so, how? If not, why?

_____

_____

_____

7. Which of the following statements is most accurate about your life?

___ I live to make myself famous and to accomplish my goals.

___ I live to make God famous and to accomplish His goals.

Based on your honest response to this question what, if anything, needs to change in your life?

_____

_____

_____

8. Many times we seek God's will in a specific area of life while living in disobedience to His Word in others. Do you believe God will show you what to do with the disobedience in your heart? Why or why not?

_____

_____

_____

THINK ABOUT THE FUTURE

"God has a wonderful way of weaving together a multitude of personal plans and purposes so that when things function according to His will, people are helping one another even as they are working with or for one another. Marriage is intended to be of mutual help. Family life is intended to be of mutual help. The church is to function in service that renders mutual help among those who are part of any particular fellowship of believers" (p. 238).

1. Complete the following statements:

   a. I am most committed in my life to

_____

_____

_____

   b. More than anything, I strive to accomplish

_____

_____

_____

What do your responses say about the importance of your relationship with God?

___ It is where it needs to be.

___ I need to reorder my priorities.

2. List five activities that take up the most time during an average day and the number of hours you spend on each activity.

ACTIVITY   HOURS

1. _____   _____

2. _____   _____

3. _____   _____

4. _____   _____

5. _____   _____

Total the hours committed to the activities above. When your schedule gets tight, what happens to your time with God?

___ I spend time with God no matter what.

___ I spend time with God when time is available.

3. If you could reorder your daily activities, what would receive top priority?

How would this adjustment affect the remainder of your day?

_____

_____

_____

What keeps you from making this your top priority?

_____

_____

_____

4. In what areas of life are you likely to accomplish only what is required?

What does this say about your desire to work for God's glory, doing your best for Him alone?

_____

_____

_____

5. Godly enthusiasm and motivation go hand in hand. You are motivated in the areas where you are enthusiastic. Based on your present condition, how motivated are you to pursue spiritual growth?

_____

_____

_____

Are there areas of life about which you are more enthusiastic than your relationship with the Lord? If so, what should you do? If not, how can you maintain your spiritual enthusiasm?

_____

_____

_____

6. Think about your time with God. What percentage is spent talking to Him versus listening to Him?

_____ % talking + _____ % listening = 100 %

If you want to discover God's will, you must spend more time listening to Him and less on talking.

7. In the space below, write what you believe the Lord's vision for your life is.

_____

_____

_____

_____

_____

_____

_____

Ask Him for help in keeping that vision when making any decision.

The Best
Is Yet to Come!

Read Chapter 12 of *How to Reach Your Full Potential for God*

Scripture Passage: Matthew 22:36–39

THINK ABOUT YOUR DIRECTION

It doesn't really matter what you want out of life: your decisions will determine where you go. You must choose to embrace your full potential and act on God's truths.

1. Think about your daily life—your relationships, hobbies, education, career path, spirituality, passions, and so forth. If you continue on the present course, how close will you come to

achieving your full potential? Use the diagram below to plot the next five years.

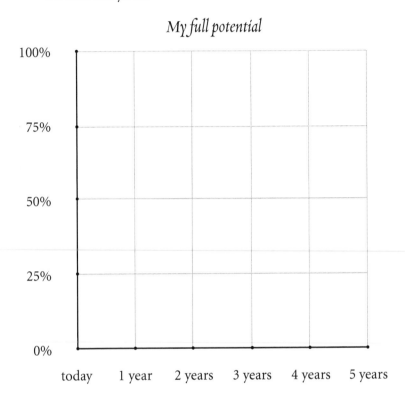

2. Are you satisfied with the progress indicated above? Why or why not?

_____

_____

_____

_____

_____

3. Do you believe the best is yet to come? Why?

_____

_____

_____

_____

4. What is the role of your relationship with God in achieving your full potential?

_____

_____

_____

_____

_____

5. "As a person with a finite mind and body, you can't begin to fathom what it will be like to live forever in an unlimited mind and body. You may have experienced great love here on this earth, but it is nothing compared to the depth of love you are going to experience in heaven. The same is true for joy and fulfillment" (pp. 244–245). How should the assurance of eternity in heaven affect your motivation now to fulfill the Lord's purposes?

_____

_____

_____

_____

_____

6. Achieving your potential begins with a passionate pursuit of God. This means you must live by His standards and principles. You must have His view of right and wrong, and make decisions based on His guidance—not your desires. For many people, this requires a radically different lifestyle. What needs to change in your life to become who God intends you to be?

_____

_____

_____

_____

_____

7. Does your heart or mind need to be cleansed by God? Explain your answer.

_____

_____

_____

_____

_____

8. To what extent are you aware of your natural abilities, ministry-related gifts, and talents? Do you need greater understanding of how to use your gifts and talents to make the Lord famous?

_____

_____

_____

_____

_____

9. How can you improve your health?

_____

_____

_____

_____

_____

10. Do any of your relationships hinder the realization of your full potential? If so, what changes do you need to make?

_____

_____

_____

_____

_____

11. How can you balance your schedule so that pursuing God is your most passionate endeavor?

_____

_____

_____

_____

_____

12. In what areas of life do you need more courage?

_____

_____

_____

_____

_____

13. Think about what influences your thoughts. How are you affected by the television shows you watch? In what way are you influenced by your music selections? How is God honored through your Internet use?

_____

_____

_____

_____

_____

14. Read **Matthew 22:36–39**. Based on an honest evaluation of your life, are you loving God with all of your heart, soul, and mind?

__ yes

__ no

15. When Jesus says to "love your neighbor as yourself," who does that include? Are you withholding love from anyone? If yes, what should you do about it?

_____

_____

_____

_____

_____

CONCLUSION

"Whatever is standing in the way of you pursuing your God-given potential with your entire heart, soul, mind, and strength, face up to it, deal with it, and ask God to work in you to make the changes you need to make, overcome the obstacles you need to overcome, and release your faith to believe for the things that lie ahead for you to receive" (p. 247). When will you make the necessary changes and begin pursuing God's full potential for your life?

___ Today (date: _____)

___ Someday

___ Never

Don't wait another day to start!

Printed in Great Britain
by Amazon